# Gratitude

*A Daily Journal*

## Honor and Appreciate
## the Abundance in Your Life

Jack Canfield *and* D.D. Watkins

**Health Communications, Inc.**
**Deerfield Beach, Florida**

*www.hcibooks.com*

**Library of Congress Cataloging-in-Publication Data
is on file with the Library of Congress.**

© 2007 D.D. Watkins and Self-Esteem Seminars LP

ISBN-10: 0-7573-0710-8
ISBN-13: 978-0-7573-0710-2

Publisher: Health Communications, Inc.
　　　　　3201 S.W. 15th Street
　　　　　Deerfield Beach, FL 33442-8190

*Introduction by Jack Canfield & D.D. Watkins*
*Cover and Graphics Design by D.D. Watkins*
*Graphics Design by Tina Renga*
*Research & Compilation by Tina Renga*
*Gratitude Cover Page Artwork by Tina Renga*
*Acknowledgment Cover Page Artwork: by D.D. Watkins*
*Cover photos (Map): ©GettyImages and BigStockPhoto.com; (rosette/key hole):*
　*Kelly Young, (Abstract Paper): Vladislav Gansovsky*

# GRATITUDE

Gratitude is a prayer.

It is a joyful and selfless expression of thankfulness from within. Whenever you are in a state of gratitude and appreciation you are in a state of natural abundance. Through gratitude and appreciation you are focusing your thoughts and energy on the beauty and abundance that is *already* present in your life. You are sending a clear message to the universe that *this* is what you would like to experience more of. There is no greater prayer than one of sincere heartfelt love, appreciation, and gratitude. These pure emotions are of the highest vibrational frequency, and through the Law of Attraction they will automatically attract even more to be thankful for. They will create a vibrational match for all the beauty and abundance that the universe has to offer.

Make a conscious decision to have an attitude of gratitude. Choose to live in a state of constant joy, gratitude, and appreciation, and acknowledge how fortunate you are. Don't take even the simplest things for granted—appreciate them and give thanks. This feeling and expression of gratitude is simply good for you. It increases your sense of well-being, awareness, enthusiasm, happiness, determination, and optimism. It raises your vibrational frequency and creates an upward-spiraling process of ever increasing joy, gratitude, and abundance that just keeps getting better and better.

## Your Gratitude Journal

Every day we have so many things to be grateful for. Your daily gratitude journal is a place to honor and acknowledge the good in your life, a place to appreciate all that you are already blessed with. Your gratitude journal will inspire you and serve as a daily reminder to focus on the positive and on the many areas of abundance in your life. By keeping a journal of all that you are grateful for, you will attract more of those things to you. It is a simple concept and a powerful tool in the deliberate creation of the life you desire.

Remember to be grateful for even the difficult and challenging situations in your life. These situations contribute to your spiritual and emotional growth, and they are often opportunities to develop a new quality, strength, skill, insight, or wisdom. Be grateful for the lessons and growth they provide.

Rise to these occasions, and appreciate all that you are learning in the process. By staying positive and appreciative through these trying times, you will avoid creating or attracting more challenging situations into your life. By learning to be grateful for even the difficulties you experience, you will positively shift your energy to the highest possible frequency. This will create a vibrational match for the positive energy and experiences that you do want to attract.

So, take the time to notice and appreciate all the good that is present in your life. This will automatically and effortlessly attract more good into your life. Make a commitment to use your gratitude journal *daily*. Take the time each evening before going to bed to review your day, and think about the events that have transpired. Become aware of how many good things actually happened, and remember to appreciate even the challenges that you encountered. Select the five things, people, or events that you are most grateful for, and write them down.

There is no right or wrong here, just write down whatever, or whoever, you are sincerely grateful for on that particular day. *Anything* you are grateful for. As you write them in your journal, really *feel* the appreciation, and give thanks. This time spent in gratitude will become a sacred part of your daily routine.

It's also a good idea to start your day in a place of gratitude. Take a few quiet moments each morning to really be thankful and to simply appreciate how fortunate you are. By doing so, you will begin each day in a state of powerful positive attraction that will set the tone for the rest of your day. If you prefer writing in your gratitude journal in the mornings, that's fine, too. The goal here is to begin and end each day with gratitude.

*Acknowledgment*

A portion of your gratitude journal is devoted solely to acknowledgment. Spend some time in quiet contemplation at the end of each day, and notice the changes that are occurring in your life. Acknowledge God's presence and the miracles all around you. Miracles can and do occur on a daily basis. Notice them, honor them, and write them down. Through your continued expressions of acknowledgment and gratitude, you will become increasingly aware of these miracles and the amazing synchronicity that is already present in your life. Use the acknowledgment portion of your journal as a place to record any specific experiences you've had that illustrate the effects of the Law of Attraction at work in your life. Since whatever you focus on expands, the more you notice it working, the more it will work.

Remember the importance of gratitude and appreciation in *all* areas of your life, and be sure to devote time daily to connect with God and with yourself. You will begin to notice a change in your perception of each day's events. You will become more aware of the positive things that happen all around you every single day. Your focus will shift, your energy will shift, and you will begin to appreciate how blessed you already are.

And . . . the Law of Attraction will respond to the higher vibration you are creating.

*I live in gratitude . . .*

*For all that I have given*
  *And for all that I've received.*
*For the beauty in my life*
  *And for the sorrows I have known.*
*For the challenges I've faced*
  *And for just how far I've come.*
*For my courage and my gifts,*
  *And for the wisdom I've acquired.*
*For the journey and experience*
  *And for kindness on the way.*
*For my dreams and my desires*
  *And for the trust that I have learned.*
*For the joy and inspiration.*
  *And for my purpose, newly found.*
*For the miracles unfolding*
  *And for what tomorrow holds.*
*For all the love I've ever known*
  *And for that I've yet to give.*
*For my friends, my home, and family*
  *And for the time to find myself.*
*For abundance and simplicity*
  *And for the grace and opportunity.*
*For the chance to make a difference*
  *And for the faith to know I will.*

                    *D.D. Watkins*

# GRATITUDE

*To those who have inspired us
along the way . . . we are grateful.*

# JANUARY

*Develop an attitude of gratitude,*
*and give thanks for everything*
*that happens to you, knowing that*
*every step forward is a step toward*
*achieving something bigger and better*
*than your current situation.*

*Brian Tracy*

*Joy is the simplest form*
*of gratitude.*

*Karl Barth*

## JANUARY 1

_____

_____

_____

_____

_____

## JANUARY 2

_____

_____

_____

_____

_____

## JANUARY 3

_____

_____

_____

_____

_____

## JANUARY 4

_____

_____

_____

_____

_____

## JANUARY 5

_____

_____

_____

_____

_____

## JANUARY 6

_____

_____

_____

_____

_____

## JANUARY 7

_____

_____

_____

_____

_____

## JANUARY 8

_____

_____

_____

_____

_____

## JANUARY 9

_____

_____

_____

_____

_____

## JANUARY 10

_____

_____

_____

_____

_____

## JANUARY 11

_____

_____

_____

_____

_____

*Gratitude helps you to grow and expand;*
*gratitude brings joy and laughter*
*into your life and into the lives of*
*all those around you.*

*Eileen Caddy*

## JANUARY 12

_____
_____
_____
_____
_____

## JANUARY 13

_____
_____
_____
_____
_____

## JANUARY 14

_____
_____
_____
_____
_____

**JANUARY 15**

_____

_____

_____

_____

_____

**JANUARY 16**

_____

_____

_____

_____

_____

**JANUARY 17**

_____

_____

_____

_____

_____

*Gratitude consists of being
more aware of what you have,
than what you don't.*

*Author Unknown*

## JANUARY 18

_____

_____

_____

_____

_____

## JANUARY 19

_____

_____

_____

_____

_____

## JANUARY 20

_____

_____

_____

_____

_____

## JANUARY 21

_____

_____

_____

_____

_____

## JANUARY 22

---
---
---
---
---

## JANUARY 23

---
---
---
---
---

## JANUARY 24

---
---
---
---
---

## JANUARY 25

---
---
---
---
---

*The essence of all beautiful art,*
*all great art, is gratitude.*

*Friedrich Nietzsche*

## JANUARY 26

_____
_____
_____

_____

_____

## JANUARY 27

_____
_____

_____

_____

_____

## JANUARY 28

_____
_____

_____

_____

_____

## JANUARY 29

_____

_____

_____

_____

_____

## JANUARY 30

_____

_____

_____

_____

_____

## JANUARY 31

_____

_____

_____

_____

_____

*Gratitude is when memory is stored
in the heart and not in the mind.*

*Lionel Hampton*

# FEBRUARY

*Gratitude unlocks the fullness of life.*
*It turns what we have into enough and*
*more. It turns denial into acceptance,*
*chaos to order, confusion to clarity.*
*It can turn a meal into a feast,*
*a house into a home,*
*a stranger into a friend.*

*Melody Beattie*

*Feeling gratitude and not expressing it is like*
*wrapping a present and not giving it.*

*William Arthur Ward*

## FEBRUARY 1

_____
_____
_____
_____
_____

## FEBRUARY 2

_____
_____
_____
_____
_____

## FEBRUARY 3

_____
_____
_____
_____
_____

## FEBRUARY 4

_____

_____

_____

_____

_____

## FEBRUARY 5

_____

_____

_____

_____

_____

## FEBRUARY 6

_____

_____

_____

_____

_____

## FEBRUARY 7

_____

_____

_____

_____

_____

## FEBRUARY 8

_____

_____

_____

_____

_____

## FEBRUARY 9

_____

_____

_____

_____

## FEBRUARY 10

_____

_____

_____

_____

## FEBRUARY 11

_____

_____

_____

_____

*God has two dwellings; one in heaven, and the other in a meek and thankful heart.*

*Izaak Walton*

## FEBRUARY 12

_____

_____

_____

_____

_____

## FEBRUARY 13

_____

_____

_____

_____

_____

## FEBRUARY 14

_____

_____

_____

_____

_____

## FEBRUARY 15

_____

_____

_____

_____

_____

## FEBRUARY 16

_____

_____

_____

_____

_____

## FEBRUARY 17

_____

_____

_____

_____

_____

*Saying thank you
is more than good manners.
It is good spirituality.*

*Alfred Painter*

## FEBRUARY 18

_____

_____

_____

_____

_____

## FEBRUARY 19

_____

_____

_____

_____

_____

## FEBRUARY 20

_____

_____

_____

_____

_____

## FEBRUARY 21

_____

_____

_____

_____

_____

## FEBRUARY 22

_____

_____

_____

_____

_____

## FEBRUARY 23

_____

_____

_____

_____

_____

## FEBRUARY 24

_____

_____

_____

_____

_____

## FEBRUARY 25

_____

_____

_____

_____

_____

*Gratitude is the fairest blossom*
*which springs from the soul.*

*Henry Ward Beecher*

## FEBRUARY 26

_____
_____
_____
_____
_____

## FEBRUARY 27

_____
_____
_____
_____

## FEBRUARY 28

_____
_____
_____
_____
_____

## FEBRUARY 29

_____

_____

_____

_____

_____

*Gratitude makes sense of our past, brings
peace for today and creates a
vision for tomorrow.*

*Melody Beattie*

# MARCH

*Joy is an attitude; it is the
presence of love—for self and others
It comes from a feeling of inner peace,
the ability to give and receive, and
appreciation of the self and others.
It is a state of gratitude and compassion,
a feeling of connection to
your higher self.*

*Unknown*

*Appreciation can make a day, even change a life.*
*Your willingness to put it into words*
*is all that is necessary.*

*Margaret Cousins*

**MARCH 1**

_____
_____
_____
_____
_____

**MARCH 2**

_____
_____
_____
_____
_____

**MARCH 3**

_____
_____
_____
_____
_____

## MARCH 4

_____

_____

_____

_____

_____

## MARCH 5

_____

_____

_____

_____

_____

## MARCH 6

_____

_____

_____

_____

_____

## MARCH 7

_____

_____

_____

_____

_____

## MARCH 8

_____

_____

_____

_____

_____

## MARCH 9

_____

_____

_____

_____

## MARCH 10

_____

_____

_____

_____

## MARCH 11

_____

_____

_____

_____

*Gratitude is the sign of noble souls.*

*Aesop Fables*

## MARCH 12

_____

_____

_____

_____

_____

## MARCH 13

_____

_____

_____

_____

_____

## MARCH 14

_____

_____

_____

_____

_____

## MARCH 15

_____

_____

_____

_____

_____

## MARCH 16

_____

_____

_____

_____

## MARCH 17

_____

_____

_____

_____

_____

*I would maintain that
thanks are the highest form of thought,
and that gratitude is happiness
doubled by wonder.*

*Gilbert K. Chesterton*

## MARCH 18

---
---
---
---
---

## MARCH 19

---
---
---
---
---

## MARCH 20

---
---
---
---
---

## MARCH 21

---
---
---
---
---

**MARCH 22**

_____

_____

_____

_____

_____

**MARCH 23**

_____

_____

_____

_____

_____

**MARCH 24**

_____

_____

_____

_____

_____

**MARCH 25**

_____

_____

_____

_____

_____

*When it comes to life, the critical thing*
*is whether you take things for granted or*
*take them with gratitude.*

*Gilbert K. Chesterton*

## MARCH 26

_____

_____

_____

_____

_____

## MARCH 27

_____

_____

_____

_____

_____

## MARCH 28

_____

_____

_____

_____

_____

## MARCH 29

_____

_____

_____

_____

_____

## MARCH 30

_____

_____

_____

_____

_____

## MARCH 31

_____

_____

_____

_____

_____

*A single grateful thought toward heaven*
*is the most complete prayer.*

*Gotthold Lessing*

# APRIL

*The riches they receive*
*will be in exact proportion to the*
*definiteness of their vision, the fixity*
*of their purpose, the steadiness of*
*their faith, and the depth*
*of their gratitude.*

*Wallace D. Wattles*

*The clearest sign of wisdom*
*is continued cheerfulness.*

*Michel Montaigne*

## APRIL 1

_____

_____

_____

_____

_____

## APRIL 2

_____

_____

_____

_____

_____

## APRIL 3

_____

_____

_____

_____

_____

## APRIL 4

_____

_____

_____

_____

_____

## APRIL 5

_____

_____

_____

_____

_____

## APRIL 6

_____

_____

_____

_____

_____

## APRIL 7

_____

_____

_____

_____

_____

## APRIL 8

_____

_____

_____

_____

_____

## APRIL 9

_____

_____

_____

_____

_____

## APRIL 10

_____

_____

_____

_____

_____

## APRIL 11

_____

_____

_____

_____

_____

*Everything we do should be*
*a result of our gratitude for what*
*God has done for us.*

*Lauryn Hill*

## APRIL 12

_____

_____

_____

_____

_____

## APRIL 13

_____

_____

_____

_____

_____

## APRIL 14

_____

_____

_____

_____

_____

## APRIL 15

_____

_____

_____

_____

_____

## APRIL 16

_____

_____

_____

_____

_____

## APRIL 17

_____

_____

_____

_____

_____

*As we express our gratitude,*
*we must never forget that the highest*
*appreciation is not to utter words,*
*but to live by them.*

*John F. Kennedy*

## APRIL 18

## APRIL 19

## APRIL 20

## APRIL 21

## APRIL 22

_____
_____
_____
_____
_____

## APRIL 23

_____
_____
_____
_____
_____

## APRIL 24

_____
_____
_____
_____
_____

## APRIL 25

_____
_____
_____
_____
_____

*One can never pay in gratitude; one can only pay "in kind" somewhere else in life.*

*Anne Morrow Lindbergh*

## APRIL 26

_____
_____
_____
_____
_____

## APRIL 27

_____
_____
_____
_____
_____

## APRIL 28

_____
_____
_____
_____
_____

## APRIL 29

_____

_____

_____

_____

_____

## APRIL 30

_____

_____

_____

_____

_____

*To find the universal elements enough;*
*to find the air and the water exhilarating; to be*
*refreshed by a morning walk or an evening saunter;*
*to be thrilled by the stars at night; to be elated*
*over a bird's nest or a wildflower in spring . . .*
*these are some of the rewards*
*of the simple life.*

*John Burroughs*

# MAY

*If you concentrate on finding
whatever is good in every situation,
you will discover that your life
will suddenly be filled with gratitude,
a feeling that nurtures the soul.*

*Harold Kushner*

*Gratitude is the most exquisite*
*form of courtesy.*

*Jacques Maritain*

**MAY 1**

_____

_____

_____

_____

_____

**MAY 2**

_____

_____

_____

_____

_____

**MAY 3**

_____

_____

_____

_____

_____

**MAY 4**

_____

_____

_____

_____

**MAY 5**

_____

_____

_____

_____

**MAY 6**

_____

_____

_____

_____

**MAY 7**

_____

_____

_____

_____

**MAY 8**

_____

_____

_____

_____

_____

**MAY 9**

_____

_____

_____

_____

_____

**MAY 10**

_____

_____

_____

_____

**MAY 11**

_____

_____

_____

_____

_____

*Happiness is itself a kind of gratitude.*

*Joseph Wood Krutch*

**MAY 12**

_____
_____
_____
_____
_____

**MAY 13**

_____
_____
_____
_____
_____

**MAY 14**

_____
_____
_____
_____

**MAY 15**

_____

_____

_____

_____

_____

**MAY 16**

_____

_____

_____

_____

_____

**MAY 17**

_____

_____

_____

_____

_____

*If the only prayer you said*
*in your whole life was thank you,*
*that would suffice.*

*Meister Eckhart*

**MAY 18**

_____

_____

_____

_____

_____

**MAY 19**

_____

_____

_____

_____

_____

**MAY 20**

_____

_____

_____

_____

_____

**MAY 21**

_____

_____

_____

_____

## MAY 22

_____

_____

_____

_____

_____

## MAY 23

_____

_____

_____

_____

_____

## MAY 24

_____

_____

_____

_____

_____

## MAY 25

_____

_____

_____

_____

_____

*The deepest craving of human nature*
*is the need to be appreciated.*

*William James*

## MAY 26

_____
_____
_____
_____
_____

## MAY 27

_____
_____
_____
_____
_____

## MAY 28

_____
_____
_____
_____
_____

**MAY 29**

_____

_____

_____

_____

_____

**MAY 30**

_____

_____

_____

_____

_____

**MAY 31**

_____

_____

_____

_____

_____

*Gratitude is heaven itself.*

*William Blake*

# JUNE

*To see the world in a grain of sand*
*and heaven in a wildflower,*
*hold infinity in the palm of your hand*
*and eternity in an hour.*

*William Blake*

*God has given us two hands, one to receive with and the other to give with.*

*Billy Graham*

## JUNE 1

_____

_____

_____

_____

_____

## JUNE 2

_____

_____

_____

_____

_____

## JUNE 3

_____

_____

_____

_____

_____

## JUNE 4

_____

_____

_____

_____

_____

## JUNE 5

_____

_____

_____

_____

_____

## JUNE 6

_____

_____

_____

_____

_____

## JUNE 7

_____

_____

_____

_____

_____

## JUNE 8

_____

_____

_____

_____

_____

## JUNE 9

_____

_____

_____

_____

_____

## JUNE 10

_____

_____

_____

_____

_____

## JUNE 11

_____

_____

_____

_____

_____

*We can only be said to be alive*
*in those moments when our hearts*
*are conscious of our treasures.*

*Thornton Wilder*

**JUNE 12**

_____
_____
_____
_____
_____

**JUNE 13**

_____
_____
_____
_____
_____

**JUNE 14**

_____
_____
_____
_____
_____

## JUNE 15

---

---

---

---

---

## JUNE 16

---

---

---

---

---

## JUNE 17

---

---

---

---

---

*There is a calmness to a life lived*
*in Gratitude, a quiet joy.*

*Ralph H. Blum*

## JUNE 18

_____

_____

_____

_____

_____

## JUNE 19

_____

_____

_____

_____

_____

## JUNE 20

_____

_____

_____

_____

_____

## JUNE 21

_____

_____

_____

_____

_____

**JUNE 22**

_____

_____

_____

_____

_____

**JUNE 23**

_____

_____

_____

_____

_____

**JUNE 24**

_____

_____

_____

_____

_____

**JUNE 25**

_____

_____

_____

_____

_____

*Living in the moment brings you a sense of*
*reverence for all of life's blessings.*

*Oprah Winfrey*

## JUNE 26

_____
_____
_____
_____
_____

## JUNE 27

_____
_____
_____
_____
_____

## JUNE 28

_____
_____
_____
_____
_____

## JUNE 29

_____
_____
_____
_____
_____

## JUNE 30

_____
_____
_____
_____
_____

*At times our own light goes out and
is rekindled by a spark from another person.
Each of us has cause to think with deep
gratitude of those who have lighted
the flame within us.*

Albert Schweitzer

# JULY

What sunshine is to
flowers, smiles are to humanity.
These are but trifles, to be sure;
but, scattered along life's pathway, the
good they do is inconceivable.

Joseph Addison

*Each day comes bearing its own gifts.*
*Untie the ribbons.*

*Ruth Ann Schabaker*

## JULY 1

_____
_____
_____
_____
_____

## JULY 2

_____
_____
_____
_____
_____

## JULY 3

_____
_____
_____
_____
_____

## JULY 4

_____

_____

_____

_____

_____

## JULY 5

_____

_____

_____

_____

_____

## JULY 6

_____

_____

_____

_____

_____

## JULY 7

_____

_____

_____

_____

_____

## JULY 8

_____

_____

_____

_____

_____

## JULY 9

_____

_____

_____

_____

_____

## JULY 10

_____

_____

_____

_____

_____

## JULY 11

_____

_____

_____

_____

_____

*I thank God for my handicaps,*
*for through them I have found myself,*
*my work, and my God.*

*Helen Keller*


## JULY 12

_____
_____
_____
_____
_____


## JULY 13

_____
_____
_____
_____
_____


## JULY 14

_____
_____
_____
_____
_____

## JULY 15

_____
_____
_____
_____
_____

## JULY 16

_____
_____
_____
_____
_____

## JULY 17

_____
_____
_____
_____
_____

*Once we discover how to appreciate the timeless values in our daily experiences, we can enjoy the best things in life.*

*Harry Hepner*

## JULY 18

---
---
---
---
---

## JULY 19

---
---
---
---
---

## JULY 20

---
---
---
---
---

## JULY 21

---
---
---
---
---

**JULY 22**

_____

_____

_____

_____

_____

**JULY 23**

_____

_____

_____

_____

_____

**JULY 24**

_____

_____

_____

_____

_____

**JULY 25**

_____

_____

_____

_____

_____

*In our daily lives, we must see
that it is not happiness that makes us
grateful, but the gratefulness that
makes us happy.*

*Albert Clarke*

**JULY 26**

_____
_____
_____
_____
_____

**JULY 27**

_____
_____
_____
_____
_____

**JULY 28**

_____
_____
_____
_____
_____

## JULY 29

_____

_____

_____

_____

## JULY 30

_____

_____

_____

_____

## JULY 31

_____

_____

_____

_____

*There are only two ways to live your life.
One is as though nothing is a miracle.
The other is as though everything
is a miracle.*

*Albert Einstein*

# AUGUST

*Happiness cannot be traveled to,*
*owned, earned, worn, or consumed.*
*Happiness is the spiritual experience*
*of living every minute with love,*
*grace, and gratitude.*

*Denis Waitley*

*Gratitude is a quality similar to electricity:*
*it must be produced and discharged and*
*used up in order to exist at all.*

*William Faulkner*

## AUGUST 1

_____
_____
_____
_____
_____

## AUGUST 2

_____
_____
_____
_____
_____

## AUGUST 3

_____
_____
_____
_____
_____

## AUGUST 4

_____

_____

_____

_____

_____

## AUGUST 5

_____

_____

_____

_____

_____

## AUGUST 6

_____

_____

_____

_____

_____

## AUGUST 7

_____

_____

_____

_____

_____

## AUGUST 8

_____

_____

_____

_____

_____

## AUGUST 9

_____

_____

_____

_____

_____

## AUGUST 10

_____

_____

_____

_____

_____

## AUGUST 11

_____

_____

_____

_____

_____

*I live in gratitude . . .*

*For all that I have given*
    *And for all that I've received.*
*For the beauty in my life*
    *And for the sorrows I have known.*
*For the challenges I've faced*
    *And for just how far I've come.*
*For my courage and my gifts,*
    *And for the wisdom I've acquired.*
*For the journey and experience*
    *And for kindness on the way.*
*For my dreams and my desires*
    *And for the trust that I have learned.*
*For the joy and inspiration.*
    *And for my purpose, newly found.*
*For the miracles unfolding*
    *And for what tomorrow holds.*
*For all the love I've ever known*
    *And for that I've yet to give.*
*For my friends, my home, and family*
    *And for the time to find myself.*
*For abundance and simplicity*
    *And for the grace and opportunity.*
*For the chance to make a difference*
    *And for the faith to know I will.*

*D.D. Watkins*

*There are no mistakes, no coincidences.*
*All events are blessings given to us to learn from.*

*Elisabeth Kubler-Ross*

## AUGUST 12

_____

_____

_____

_____

_____

## AUGUST 13

_____

_____

_____

_____

_____

## AUGUST 14

_____

_____

_____

_____

_____

## AUGUST 15

_____

_____

_____

_____

_____


## AUGUST 16

_____

_____

_____

_____


## AUGUST 17

_____

_____

_____

_____


*Look at everything as though you
were seeing it either for the first or last time.
Then, your time on earth will
be filled with glory.*

*Betty Smith*

## AUGUST 18

_____

_____

_____

_____

_____

## AUGUST 19

_____

_____

_____

_____

## AUGUST 20

_____

_____

_____

_____

## AUGUST 21

_____

_____

_____

_____

## AUGUST 22

_____

_____

_____

_____

_____

## AUGUST 23

_____

_____

_____

_____

## AUGUST 24

_____

_____

_____

_____

## AUGUST 25

_____

_____

_____

_____

_____

*Those who are awake live in a*
*state of constant amazement.*

*Jack Kornfield*

## AUGUST 26

_____

_____

_____

_____

_____

## AUGUST 27

_____

_____

_____

_____

_____

## AUGUST 28

_____

_____

_____

_____

_____

## AUGUST 29

_____

_____

_____

_____

_____

## AUGUST 30

_____

_____

_____

_____

_____

## AUGUST 31

_____

_____

_____

_____

_____

*Cherish yesterday,*
*dream tomorrow,*
*live today.*

*Richard Bach*

# SEPTEMBER

*It is a glorious privilege to live,
to know, to act, to listen, to behold, to love.
To look up at the blue summer sky; to see
the sun sink slowly beyond the line
of the horizon; to watch the worlds come
twinkling into view, first one by one, and
the myriads that no man can count, and lo!
The universe is white with them;
and you and I are here.*

*Marco Morrow*

*Thankfulness is measured by the number*
*of words; gratitude is measured by*
*the nature of our actions.*

*David McKay*

## SEPTEMBER 1

_____
_____
_____
_____
_____

## SEPTEMBER 2

_____
_____
_____
_____
_____

## SEPTEMBER 3

_____
_____
_____
_____
_____

## SEPTEMBER 4

_____
_____
_____
_____
_____

## SEPTEMBER 5

_____
_____
_____
_____
_____

## SEPTEMBER 6

_____
_____
_____
_____
_____

## SEPTEMBER 7

_____
_____
_____
_____
_____

## SEPTEMBER 8

_____

_____

_____

_____

_____

## SEPTEMBER 9

_____

_____

_____

_____

_____

## SEPTEMBER 10

_____

_____

_____

_____

_____

## SEPTEMBER 11

_____

_____

_____

_____

_____

*Courtesies of a small and trivial character*
*are the ones which strike deepest in the grateful*
*and appreciating heart.*

*Henry Clay*

## SEPTEMBER 12

_____
_____
_____
_____
_____

## SEPTEMBER 13

_____
_____
_____
_____
_____

## SEPTEMBER 14

_____
_____
_____
_____

## SEPTEMBER 15

_____
_____
_____
_____
_____

## SEPTEMBER 16

_____
_____
_____
_____

## SEPTEMBER 17

_____
_____
_____
_____

*Two kinds of gratitude:*
*The sudden kind we feel for what we take;*
*the larger kind we feel for what we give.*

*Edward Arlington Robinson*

## SEPTEMBER 18

_____

_____

_____

_____

_____

## SEPTEMBER 19

_____

_____

_____

_____

_____

## SEPTEMBER 20

_____

_____

_____

_____

_____

## SEPTEMBER 21

_____

_____

_____

_____

_____

## SEPTEMBER 22

## SEPTEMBER 23

## SEPTEMBER 24

## SEPTEMBER 25

*Gratitude is not only the greatest of virtues,*
*but the parent of all the others.*

*Marcus Tullius Cicero*

## SEPTEMBER 26

_____
_____
_____
_____
_____

## SEPTEMBER 27

_____
_____
_____
_____
_____

## SEPTEMBER 28

_____
_____
_____
_____
_____

## SEPTEMBER 29

_____

_____

_____

_____

_____

## SEPTEMBER 30

_____

_____

_____

_____

_____

*The law of gratitude is universal.*
*It is a natural function of the soul.*
*All things upon this earth or in the universe*
*operate and respond to love and praise.*

*Robert Scheid*

# OCTOBER

*What a joy it is to feel the soft,*
*springy earth under my feet once more,*
*to follow grassy roads that lead to*
*ferny brooks where I can bathe my*
*fingers in a cataract of rippling notes,*
*or to clamber over a stone wall into*
*green fields that tumble and roll and*
*climb in riotous gladness!*

*Helen Keller*

*Be glad of life because it gives you*
*a chance to love and to work and to play*
*and to look up at stars.*

*Henry van Dyke*

## OCTOBER 1

_____
_____
_____
_____
_____

## OCTOBER 2

_____
_____
_____
_____
_____

## OCTOBER 3

_____
_____
_____
_____
_____

## OCTOBER 4

_____

_____

_____

_____

_____

## OCTOBER 5

_____

_____

_____

_____

_____

## OCTOBER 6

_____

_____

_____

_____

_____

## OCTOBER 7

_____

_____

_____

_____

_____

## OCTOBER 8

_____
_____
_____
_____
_____

## OCTOBER 9

_____
_____
_____
_____
_____

## OCTOBER 10

_____
_____
_____
_____
_____

## OCTOBER 11

_____
_____
_____
_____
_____

*Love wholeheartedly, be surprised,*
*give thanks and praise — then you will*
*discover the fullness of your life.*

*Brother David Steindl-Rast*

## OCTOBER 12

_____
_____
_____
_____
_____

## OCTOBER 13

_____
_____
_____
_____
_____

## OCTOBER 14

_____
_____
_____
_____
_____

## OCTOBER 15

_____
_____
_____
_____
_____

## OCTOBER 16

_____
_____
_____
_____
_____

## OCTOBER 17

_____
_____
_____
_____
_____

*One who Gives is One who Lives
a life of Gratitude. Choose the Attitude.
Elevate your Spiritual Latitude.*

*Leela Vox*

## OCTOBER 18

_____
_____
_____
_____
_____

## OCTOBER 19

_____
_____
_____
_____
_____

## OCTOBER 20

_____
_____
_____
_____
_____

## OCTOBER 21

_____
_____
_____
_____
_____

## OCTOBER 22

_____

_____

_____

_____

_____

## OCTOBER 23

_____

_____

_____

_____

_____

## OCTOBER 24

_____

_____

_____

_____

_____

## OCTOBER 25

_____

_____

_____

_____

_____

*Praise, or gratitude, is love*
*or faith in action.*

*Robert Scheid*

## OCTOBER 26

_____
_____
_____
_____
_____

## OCTOBER 27

_____
_____
_____
_____
_____

## OCTOBER 28

_____
_____
_____
_____
_____

## OCTOBER 29

_____
_____
_____
_____
_____

## OCTOBER 30

_____
_____
_____
_____

## OCTOBER 31

_____
_____
_____
_____

*If Existence was ever*
*a miracle, then existence is*
*always a miracle.*

*Andrew Schwartz*

# NOVEMBER

*There is only one thing that can
form a bond between men, and that is
gratitude . . . we cannot give someone
else greater power over us than
we have ourselves.*

*Charles de Secondat*

*He is a wise man who does not*
*grieve for the things which he has not,*
*but rejoices for those which he has.*

*Epictetus*

## NOVEMBER 1

_____

_____

_____

_____

_____

## NOVEMBER 2

_____

_____

_____

_____

_____

## NOVEMBER 3

_____

_____

_____

_____

_____

## NOVEMBER 4

_____

_____

_____

_____

_____

## NOVEMBER 5

_____

_____

_____

_____

_____

## NOVEMBER 6

_____

_____

_____

_____

_____

## NOVEMBER 7

_____

_____

_____

_____

_____

## NOVEMBER 8

## NOVEMBER 9

## NOVEMBER 10

## NOVEMBER 11

*I awoke this morning with devout*
*thanksgiving for my friends,*
*the old and the new.*

*Ralph Waldo Emerson*

## NOVEMBER 12

_____

_____

_____

_____

_____

## NOVEMBER 13

_____

_____

_____

_____

_____

## NOVEMBER 14

_____

_____

_____

_____

_____

## NOVEMBER 15

_____

## NOVEMBER 16

_____

## NOVEMBER 17

_____

*The heart is always the place to go.*
*Go home into your heart, where there is warmth,*
*appreciation, gratitude, and contentment.*

*Ayya Khema*

## NOVEMBER 18

## NOVEMBER 19

## NOVEMBER 20

## NOVEMBER 21

## NOVEMBER 22

_____

_____

_____

_____

_____

## NOVEMBER 23

_____

_____

_____

_____

## NOVEMBER 24

_____

_____

_____

_____

## NOVEMBER 25

_____

_____

_____

_____

*The hardest arithmetic to master*
*is that which enables us to*
*count our blessings.*

*Eric Hoffer*

## NOVEMBER 26

_____
_____
_____
_____
_____

## NOVEMBER 27

_____
_____
_____
_____
_____

## NOVEMBER 28

_____
_____
_____
_____

## NOVEMBER 29

_____

_____

_____

_____

_____

## NOVEMBER 30

_____

_____

_____

_____

_____

*Feeling grateful or appreciative
of someone or something in your life
actually attracts more of the things that
you appreciate and value
into your life.*

*Christiane Northrup*

# DECEMBER

*If future generations are to
remember us more with gratitude
than sorrow, we must achieve more than
just the miracles of technology.
We must also leave them a glimpse
of the world as it was created, not
just as it looked when we
got through with it.*

*Lyndon B. Johnson*

*Let's be grateful for those who*
*give us happiness; they are the charming*
*gardeners who make our soul bloom*

*Marcel Proust*

## DECEMBER 1

_____
_____
_____
_____
_____

## DECEMBER 2

_____
_____
_____
_____
_____

## DECEMBER 3

_____
_____
_____
_____
_____

## DECEMBER 4

## DECEMBER 5

## DECEMBER 6

## DECEMBER 7

## DECEMBER 8

_____

_____

_____

_____

_____

## DECEMBER 9

_____

_____

_____

_____

_____

## DECEMBER 10

_____

_____

_____

_____

_____

## DECEMBER 11

_____

_____

_____

_____

_____

*It isn't the big pleasures that*
*count the most; it's making a great*
*deal out of the little ones.*

*Jean Webster*

## DECEMBER 12

_____
_____
_____
_____
_____

## DECEMBER 13

_____
_____
_____
_____
_____

## DECEMBER 14

_____
_____
_____
_____
_____

## DECEMBER 15

_____

_____

_____

_____

_____

## DECEMBER 16

_____

_____

_____

_____

_____

## DECEMBER 17

_____

_____

_____

_____

_____

*For today and its blessings,*
*I owe the world*
*an attitude of gratitude.*

*Clarence E. Hodges*

## DECEMBER 18

_____

_____
_____

_____

_____

## DECEMBER 19

_____

_____
_____

_____

_____

## DECEMBER 20

_____

_____
_____

_____

_____

## DECEMBER 21

_____

_____
_____

_____

_____

## DECEMBER 22

_____
_____
_____
_____
_____

## DECEMBER 23

_____
_____
_____
_____
_____

## DECEMBER 24

_____
_____
_____
_____

## DECEMBER 25

_____
_____
_____
_____

*Be grateful for the home you*
*have, knowing that at this moment,*
*all you have is all you need.*

*Sarah Ban Breathnach*

## DECEMBER 26

_____
_____
_____
_____
_____

## DECEMBER 27

_____
_____
_____
_____
_____

## DECEMBER 28

_____
_____
_____
_____
_____

## DECEMBER 29

_____

_____

_____

_____

_____


## DECEMBER 30

_____

_____

_____

_____

_____


## DECEMBER 31

_____

_____

_____

_____

_____


_I am beginning to learn that it
is the sweet, simple things of life which
are the real ones after all._

_Laura Ingalls Wilder_

# ACKNOWLEDGMENT